Pushing and Pulling

Kay Davies
and
Wendy Oldfield

Wayland

Starting Science

Books in the series

Animals
Day and Night
Electricity and Magnetism
Floating and Sinking
Food
Hot and Cold
Information Technology
Light
Local Ecology
Materials

Plants
Pushing and Pulling
Rocks and Soil
The Senses
Skeletons and Movement
Sound and Music
Time and Change
Waste
Water
Weather

About this book

Pushing and Pulling investigates the many forces involved in making objects move. Activities using spinning, rolling and sudden stops and starts are included to demonstrate these forces. Through using levers and pulleys, children learn how simple machines make lifting easy.

The investigations are designed to be straightforward but fun, and flexible according to the abilities of the children. The main picture and its commentary may be taken as an introduction to the topic or as a focal point for further discussion. Each chapter can form a basis for extended topic work.

Teachers will find that in using this book, they are reinforcing the other core subjects of language and mathematics. Through its topic approach *Pushing and Pulling* covers aspects of the National Science Curriculum for key stage 1 (levels 1 to 3), for the following Attainment Targets: Exploration of science (AT 1), Types and uses of materials (AT 6), Forces (AT 10) and Energy (AT 13). The forces which govern floating and sinking are covered in a separate book.

First published in 1992 by
Wayland (Publishers) Ltd
61 Western Road, Hove
East Sussex, BN3 1JD, England

© Copyright 1992 Wayland (Publishers) Ltd

Typeset by Kalligraphic Design Ltd, Horley,
  Surrey
Printed in Italy by Rotolito Lombarda
  S.p.A., Milan
Bound in Belgium by Casterman S.A.

**British Library Cataloguing in
  Publication Data**
Davies, Kay, 1946–
  Pushing and pulling
  I. Title   II. Oldfield, Wendy   III. Series
  612.76

ISBN 0 7502 0310 2

Book editor: Cath Senker
Series editor: Cally Chambers

CONTENTS

All fall down   5
Balancing act   6
Roundabout and out   9
In a spin   10
Hold tight!   12
Slip or grip   14
Freewheel   17
Oiling the wheels   18
Ball of energy   21
Springs in the air   23
Swing along   25
See-saw   27
Roll over   28

Glossary   30

Finding out more   31

Index   32

All the words that first appear in **bold** in the text, are explained in the glossary.

This woman has jumped out of an aeroplane with a
parachute. She falls towards the ground below.

ALL FALL DOWN

Every time you drop something it falls downwards. Our planet Earth always wants to pull things towards its centre. This force is called **gravity**.

Drop a ping-pong ball and a bouncy ball from the same height.

Do they hit the floor at the same time?

Drop other objects of the same size and shape but different **weights**.
Do they all hit the floor at the same time?

Drop a marble from different heights into a tray of sand.
Look at the dents it makes in the sand.

Are the dents bigger or smaller when you drop your marble from higher in the air?

BALANCING ACT

Can you stand on one leg without falling over?

Try with your arms stretched out. Is it easier like that?

You still wobble, but moving your arms helps you to keep **upright** on one spot.

Using your arms helps you keep your **balance**.

Make a kelly doll using an eggshell.

Empty egg shell

Stick the clay with glue

Glue the top edges

Two paper triangles

Flick the kelly doll

Glue some clay inside the bottom of the eggshell.

Paint it on the outside. Make a little paper hat.

Flick your kelly doll to try and knock it over.

The heavy weight pulls your doll upright.

Acrobats are very good at balancing. The girl in the air
has learnt to balance upside-down.

The sugar spins fast around the **revolving** drum. It is thrown against the sides and collects in sweet, sticky strands. This is candy floss!

ROUNDABOUT AND OUT

Roundabouts spin you round and round.
As they get faster you grip the bars tightly. Why?

What would happen if you let go?

The faster you spin the more you fool gravity.

Instead of falling to the ground, spinning pulls you up and outwards.

Half fill a small basket with confetti. Tie a string to the handle. Give yourself plenty of room.

Hold the string tightly and spin the basket round your head.

What happens to the basket?

What happens to the confetti?

What happens if you stop spinning the basket?

IN A SPIN

When you spin a top, a special kind of **force** makes the top spin on one spot.

This force works through the centre of the top and keeps it upright.

When the top slows down this force no longer works.

The top starts to wobble and then falls over.

Flick your top. Does it stop? Does it keep spinning in the same direction?
Once an object is spinning it always wants to move the same way.

Make a top.

Card circle

Make a hole with a pencil.

Push a used matchstick through.

Spin your top.

The ice skater spins on the ice. Her body turns very quickly to keep her spinning on one spot.

HOLD TIGHT!

It takes a lot of effort to start things moving. It's hard to stop them too.

If you're standing on a bus when it suddenly moves forwards you fall backwards. Your body doesn't want to move.

If the bus stops suddenly, you move forwards. Your body doesn't want to stop.

Find a toy truck and put a marble at the front near the driver's cab.

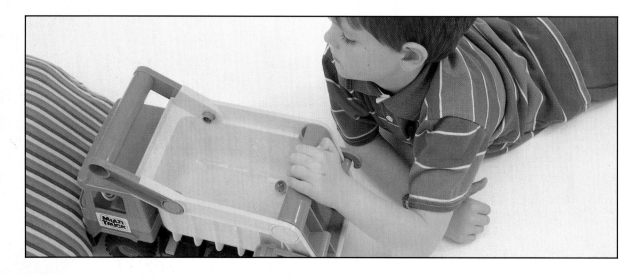

Push the truck. What happens to the marble?
Put a marble at the back of the truck. Push the truck hard into a cushion.

What happens to the marble now?

Seat belts stop our bodies moving forwards when the car stops suddenly. They protect us from being hurt.

SLIP OR GRIP

Friction is a force that works when two **surfaces** rub together. Without it, many things could not move. Friction helps things **grip**, so they can push or pull.

Look at the soles of different shoes. Guess which sole gives the best grip.

Make a slope with a board and some books.

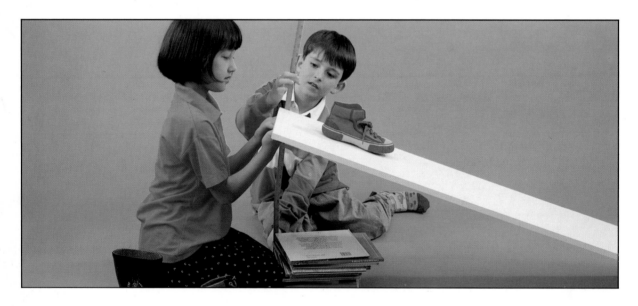

Put one of the shoes at the top of the slope.
Raise the board until the shoe starts to move.

Try this with each shoe. Measure the height at the top of the slope each time.

Which shoe gripped best? Was your guess right?
Do rough or smooth soles give the best grip?

It is hard to climb up a slide. The soles on the boy's shoes help him to get a grip.

Robert has put weeds into the wheelbarrow. The turning wheel makes the wheelbarrow easy to move.

FREEWHEEL

Could a car move easily on square wheels?

Roll a coin and a marble across a table.

Do they both move easily? Are they both round shapes?

Try rolling a dice or a sugar cube. Do they move as easily as the round shapes?

Make a ladybird roller.

Use half a walnut shell or a **papier mâché** shell made round a ball of clay.

Paint the shell red with black spots. Put a big marble under the shell.

Does your ladybird roller run on its own down a slope?

OILING THE WHEELS

There are lots of ways to make things move against each other more easily. We can use oil or soap.

Washing hands with soap

Oiling a hinge

We can use balls too. Bicycle wheels have **ball bearings** inside their **axles**. These let the wheels turn without wearing the metal axles.

Find a round tin lid. Put a heavy book on the rim and try to spin it.

Now put some marbles in your lid. They must be higher than the rim.

Put the book on top of the marbles. Spin your book. Does it spin well?

The **sweepers** polish the ice with brushes. This helps the
curling stones slip more easily over the ice.

The basketball player bounces the ball and runs. He tries to bounce the ball all the way to the basket.

BALL OF ENERGY

Drop a tennis ball on the ground. Does it bounce back?

Throw the ball at the ground. Does it bounce higher now?

The ball has more **energy** this time. The extra energy comes from the movement of your arm.

Soak a tennis ball in paint. Throw it on to some white paper and let it bounce a few times.

Measure the distance between the bounce marks. Is your ball losing energy as it bounces?

Jumping on a pogo stick squashes the spring. The spring pushes Duncan up into the air.

SPRINGS IN THE AIR

Squash a spring between your hands.
What can you feel? Let go of the spring. What
happens? Can you see why it is called a spring?

Make a Jill-in-the-jar.

Find two large hair rollers
with springs inside.
Join them together with
thin wire.

Make a puppet head
from a ping-pong ball.
Glue it on to the middle
of a round piece of cloth.

Stick felt hands to the
cloth. Tie the cloth
puppet around the springs.

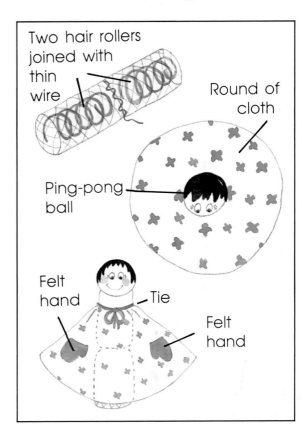

Two hair rollers joined with thin wire

Round of cloth

Ping-pong ball

Felt hand

Tie

Felt hand

Squash Jill into a small jar
with a screw top.

Unscrew the top to
watch Jill spring out.

The concrete ball swings on a chain. It crashes into the building and smashes the bricks.

SWING ALONG

A **pendulum** swings backwards and forwards.
A push will start it, but it will soon stop.

A wound-up spring or electricity keeps a pendulum going longer and can work a clock.

Fasten a ball to a piece of cord.
Hold the cord in your hand and push the ball.

How long does it swing for? Do big swings take longer than short swings?

Make painted skittles from empty plastic bottles.

Hang your ball and cord from a string above the skittles.

Swing the ball to knock your skittles down.

Pushing against the ground on a see-saw makes the other person go up in the air.

SEE-SAW

A see-saw is a **lever**. Levers help make heavy objects easy to lift.

Make a woodpecker.

Cut two slits opposite each other on a toilet roll. Make two holes opposite each other in the card, lower than the top of the slits.

Pass a thin straw through one hole, then through a thick straw, then out the other side.

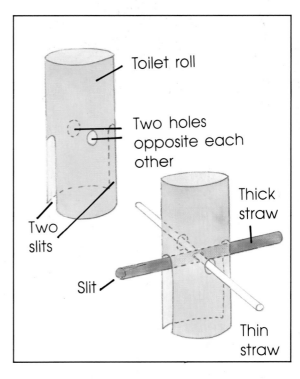

Toilet roll

Two holes opposite each other

Thick straw

Two slits

Slit

Thin straw

Cut a slit in the thick straw. Make a card woodpecker to fit into the slit.

Paint the roll to look like a tree.

Push the lever to make your woodpecker peck the tree.

ROLL OVER

Lifting heavy weights high into the air is hard.
Fill a small bucket with toys. How high can you lift it?
A **pulley** can help you.

Pass a paintbrush through a cotton reel.

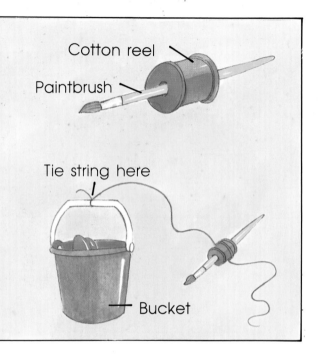

Cotton reel
Paintbrush

Fasten a long piece of string to the middle of the handle of the bucket.

Tie string here

Pass it over the cotton reel twice.

Bucket

Ask a tall friend to hold the paintbrush as high as she can.

Pull the string to lift the bucket.
How high can you lift it now?

Is it easier using your pulley?

The pullies on the boat help the sailors lift the heavy sail high into the air.

GLOSSARY

Axle A rod that goes through the centre of a wheel.

Balance To keep steady, without falling over.

Ball bearings Tiny metal balls in the axle of a wheel.

Curling stones Flat, heavy stones which are slid across the ice in the game of curling.

Energy The strength to do things.

Force The push or pull needed to move things.

Friction The force between two surfaces that makes them grip so they can push or pull. It slows things down when they are moving.

Gravity The force that pulls everything down towards the centre of the Earth.

Grip To hold tight.

Lever A simple machine for lifting loads.

Papier mâché Pieces of paper covered with glue which harden into a shape when dry.

Pendulum A weight, hanging from a thread or rod, that can swing freely.

Pulley A wheel with a rope or string round it, used for lifting a hanging load.

Revolving Turning round and round.

Surfaces The outside of objects.

Sweepers People who brush the ice in a game of curling.

Upright Standing straight.

Weight How heavy something is.

FINDING OUT MORE

Books to read:

Balls and Balloons by Ed Catherall (Wayland, 1985)
Floating and Sinking by Kay Davies and Wendy Oldfield (Wayland, 1990)
Machines by John Williams (Wayland, 1991)
Move It! by Henry Pluckrose (Franklin Watts, 1989)
My Balloon (1989), **My Boat** (1990), **My Car** (1991) by Kay Davies and Wendy Oldfield (A & C Black *Simple Science* series)
Toy Box Science by Chris Ollerenshaw and Pat Triggs (A & C Black, 1991)
Wheels by John Williams (Wayland, 1991)

Teachers' resource:

Energy, Air and Water by Terry Jennings (Scholastic, 1990)

PICTURE ACKNOWLEDGEMENTS

Allsport (D. Leah) 19, (M. Powell) 20, (B. Martin) 29; Chapel Studios 7, 8, 9 (top), 15; D. Cumming 22; Isabel Lilly 16; Photri 11; Wayland Picture Library (Zul Mukhida) cover, 5 (both), 6, 9 (bottom), 10, 12, 14, 17, 18, 21 (both), 23, 25 (both), 27, 28, (A. Blackburn) 13, 26: ZEFA 4, 24 (G. Mabbs).

Artwork illustrations by Rebecca Archer.

The publishers would also like to thank The Fold and Deepdene schools, Hove, East Sussex, for their kind co-operation.

INDEX

Acrobats 7
Axles 18, 30

Balance 6, 7, 30
Ball bearings 18, 30
Balls 5, 17, 18, 20, 21, 24, 25
Basketball 20
Bouncing 21

Candy floss 8
Curling stones 19, 30

Energy 21, 30

Force 10, 14, 30
Friction 14, 30

Gravity 5, 9, 30
Grip 9, 14, 15, 30

Ice skater 11

Jill-in-the-jar 23

Kelly doll 6

Ladybird roller 17
Levers 27, 30

Marbles 5, 12, 17, 18
Movement 12, 13, 14, 16, 17, 18

Papier mâché 17, 30
Parachute 4
Pendulum 25, 30
Pogo stick 22
Pulley 28, 29, 30
Pulling 9, 14, 28
Pushing 12, 22, 25

Revolving 8, 30
Rolling 17, 28
Roundabout 9

Sailing 29
Seat belts 13
See-saw 26, 27
Shoes 14, 15
Skittles 25
Slide 15
Slope 14, 17
Spinning 8, 9, 10-11, 18
Springs 22, 23
Surfaces 14, 30
Sweepers 19, 30
Swinging 24, 25

Top 10
Truck 12

Wheelbarrow 16
Wheels 16, 17, 18
Woodpecker 27